LOSING MY MARBLES

Trader Faulkner with John Goodwin

# LOSING MY MARBLES

How an Actor Learnt the Hard Way
A One Man Show

OBERON BOOKS
LONDON

WWW.OBERONBOOKS.COM

First published in 2003 by Oberon Books Ltd
521 Caledonian Road, London N7 9RH
Tel: +44 (0) 20 7607 3637 / Fax: +44 (0) 20 7607 3629
e-mail: info@oberonbooks.com
www.oberonbooks.com

A catalogue record for this book is available from the British
Library.

PB ISBN: 9781840022421

Visit www.oberonbooks.com to read more about all our books and to
buy them. You will also find features, author interviews and news of
any author events, and you can sign up for e-newsletters so that you're
always first to hear about our new releases.

# Contents

# Acknowledgements

In 1997, Martin Amis bestowed on me the morbid honour of giving my name to the chief murder suspect in his novel *Night Train.* Shortly after publication, I received a call from a reporter on *The Times* enquiring whether I was still alive. I was able to reassure him. But I *am* losing my marbles.

*Marbles* is a series of true stories from my life, in which the heartaches and follies of my younger days are transformed into comedy and tragedy – if you can call the inevitable calamities of youth tragedy.

The result has become an evening in the theatre during which people can forget their own troubles and laugh at mine. The show can be played anywhere there is an audience for a good story.

The staging of *Losing My Marbles* was made possible through the generosity and help of the following people, who have contributed, either financially, or by typing the various drafts until a playable text emerged, or by giving their time and encouragement.

I am indebted to Julia Fortescue through whom it all began. My grateful thanks as well to Denise Adeane, Julia Bonas, Therese Clancy, Joan and Ann Davis, Liz Drown, The Hon Seymour Fortescue, Helena Hiard, Alix Kirsta, Jesus Mora del Rio, Simon and Jane Mounsey, Isabelle Neimon, Freddy and Helia Nicolle, Jean Nysen, Phillips Photographic, Sarah Roberts, Frances Stonor Saunders, Pam Taylor, John Travis, Peter Vettesey, John Zieger.

To the aforementioned, and to others who wish to remain anonymous, without whose support my marbles would have remained safe and sterile in my pocket, I can only say, 'Who isn't wealthy to have such friends as these!'

*Losing My Marbles* was first performed at the Jermyn Street Theatre, London on 31 January 1999.

Trader Faulkner

# Setting the Scene

*Stacked upstage centre, one in front of the other, are nine large black-and-white photographs and two cartoons, all with their backs to the audience. The photographs – though not the two cartoons – are all of people featured in the stories: Peter Finch, a girl called Trixie, Trader's mother dancing in a film, the girl he calls by the nom-de-plume Marion Harkness, John Gielgud, Laurence Olivier, Vivien Leigh, Antonio – the great Spanish dancer, and Picasso. As each person is described, TRADER turns their photo round to face the audience until finally they form a line across the back of the stage.*

*The first cartoon shows a young satyr who is tormenting his elderly father; the second a torero in the bullring who just avoids being gored by the bull.*

*Already on stage are a high stool, and a pair of ancient Spanish flamenco boots.*

*TRADER enters to Cuban music. He welcomes the audience to the show and ad-libs briefly into the first story...*

# Losing My Marbles

'You were nine months of purgatory, nine hours of hell, and a lifetime trying to rear a dunderhead.' That's Mum's description of my arrival, and after.

She and Dad were English born and bred and I loved them both. But I was born Down Under, where acceptance among your peers meant you had to be an ace at cricket and rugby, with a capacity to tank up on lager…schooners of it.

My first school was the local state school at Sydney's surfing paradise, Manly. And we seven- to eight-year-olds were Manly's riff raff. The school was known as the Manly Public School – the Manly Pubic to us kids. It was there, aged seven, that I had my initiation into the obscenities of Australiana.

In my class were Billy Barber, Ray Harney, Alic Lecky, Mike Hunt (try saying that quickly), Poofta Sykes, very effeminate with large adenoids, and Tusker Mackintosh, his two front teeth gone and a crew cut on a head that resembled a mallee root.

The Manly girls were just as wicked: Lorna Wunderlick, Stella Godbolt, Emma Hazel Royds (Emmeroids to us), and a hot little sheila called Norma Tryke. She was dead wicked. Chalked up on the wall of the boys' dunny was: 'Norma Trike is the Town Bike. Who's for a Naked Roide? Thrills and Spills on the Hot Seat.' In those sweltering summers we kids went around half naked, and in a deserted paddock Norma was ever ready to display her nubile charms by offering us boys 'a niked roide'.

Marbles was all the rage at that school. You had to knock out of a circle, drawn in the dirt, as many as possible of your opponent's marbles – or 'goolies'. You did this by flicking in one of your own. Dad bought me a hundred goolies. I lost the lot. Far worse, I lost face.

'No uthe thtanding there loike a one-legged man at an arthe kickin contetht,' yelled Tusker. 'Gow hown an git th'more goolies.'

Home I ran. But nothing could induce Dad to invest further in goolies. My Dad was never a soft touch. A hard-drinking, gregarious, womanising movie actor, his bar-room cronies called him Jack the Rattler, a reference to his one-eyed trouser snake. Back in the 1930s Depression the once flourishing Australian film industry had crashed with Wall Street, and Dad was on the skids. But he kept us off poverty row by distilling an illicit gut-rot in the bath and flogging it to his Freemason colleagues. He called it Rattler's Whisky, and if any of this hooch remained in the bath after the old alchemist had bottled what he needed, the bathroom was always locked.

The day he refused me more money for marbles, Dad had left some of this gut-rot in the bottom of the bath. Now a builder's ladder – my lucky day – was propped up against the outside wall of our block of flats. Why couldn't I nip up through our bathroom window, and fill some empty ginger beer bottles with Rattler's Whisky? These I could trade at school for my lost goolies.

Up I scuttled like a rat up a drainpipe, my satchel full of empty bottles. In no time I was down with five of them filled to the brim. At twenty goolies a bottle, I'd be sure to regain my lost pride – and my hundred goolies.

Next morning Tusker waylaid me. 'Gotcha goolies, sport?'

'I've got five bottles of Dad's best whisky. Couple of swigs of that an ya nuts'll drop. It's twenty goolies a bottle. Five goolies a snort. And one goolie a sniff.'

Ray Harney parted with one goolie and took a sniff… 'Strewth!'

Poofta Sykes took a mega whiff and had to cough up two goolies. 'Jeez…what a stink! …Lay ya flat like a lizard drinkin'.'

'G'us a swig Rono.' Rono was the Aussie abbreviation of my name, Ronald.

Quick as a flash I got back my hundred goolies and we weaved our way back to our desks like a swarm of swatted flies.

Rodney Bottomly was to read to the class *How Horatio Held the Bridge.* But we never discovered how. Rodney lurched to his feet, turned cholera yellow, and did a technicolor yawn all over his desk. The heavy guzzlers now started crashing like skittles in a bowling alley. Those too pissed to stay vertical were rushed to the Manly District Hospital to be stomach-pumped. Dad was summoned to remove me and told I'd traded his precious Rattler's for marbles.

*Reveals cartoon of two satyrs: an old man blocking his ears as a young boy makes excruciating sounds on his pan pipes. Both have horns, but the young boy's look like two marbles on his forehead.*

Puce with rage Dad marched me home. I was walloped with his razor strap, and the school expelled me.

'The only possible school for you, my lad,' growled Dad, 'is the reformatory,' adding, 'I seem to have spawned a right little Trader.' The name stuck.

# Finchie's Trick

School and I parted company just as the Second World War was coming to an end. I was free to realise my life's ambition to join the Royal Australian Navy. They turned me down… underweight. I had a second go with lead balls in my trouser pockets. That put my weight up a stone.

'But you're as thin as a Hong Kong chopstick,' said the Naval medico. 'What's that bulge in your trousers? It can't be your testicles. Get back on the scales…stripped.' I was exposed.

With neither rudder nor compass I took on one job after another. As an office boy at Lever Bros to be groomed for executive status – a business executive? Me? I was a disaster. I tried manual labour, clearing scrub land for building sites, got muscle cramps and was sacked. As a Lifesaver on Manly beach I dived into the surf to save a very fat lady caught in an undertow and almost drowned us both.

Then an encounter at Sydney's cosmopolitan coffee bar Repins suddenly gave my life direction. There I met that self-styled gypsy character irresistible to so many women, Peter Finch.

*Reveals photo.*

Aint ee beut? Idolised by those of us in Sydney he trained to act.

Back in 1935, Finchie, as we all called him, had played the juvenile in the drama group of a travelling circus, run by an aboriginal impresario, that toured the Australian Outback. His mates in the circus were the Flying Ardinis, a family of trapeze artists. Now – thirteen years later – Ted Ardini was teaching acrobatics in Sydney, and Peter was our top actor and not a bad director, though not yet a movie star.

Finchie decided that I was ideal material on which to try out his production notions: 'At eighteen you can learn to act with your body as well as with your voice. To use your body like an acrobat. Will you be my guinea pig?'

'Oh yeah, that'd be great,' said I.

'But,' Finchie added, 'you've got to be able to do the acrobatic basic – the back-flip. Deliberately losing balance, you somersault backwards in an arc on to your hands. Then you spring off your hands on to your feet again. Mistime that and you end up with a fractured spine or a broken neck,' – or, as Finchie put it – 'blowing your nose through your bum.'

Ted Ardini put me through the acrobat's torture of spine-pulling and limb manipulation. Finchie stayed away. He also stayed away over the months my aching body, strapped in a harness, was flipped safely over, with Ted and the harness always taking my weight.

Came the day Finchie arrived.

'Tonight,' he said, 'this Emu will fly.' Ted fitted the harness. The Emu preened his plumage. Ho… HuuuuP.

Ted jerked the harness. I was over and back on my feet before Finchie could blink.

'Okay,' he said, 'now take off the harness.'

I took up my position on the mat, and flung my arms downwards ready to leap. It didn't happen. My next leap could be into a wheelchair.

'Go for it, Trade. You can do it lad,' shouted Ted. The Emu stood there, stricken. Finchie tried bribery, promising to cast me as a back-flipping Puck, and as Ariel in *The Tempest* spiralling into space on invisible wires. Abject funk rooted me to the spot.

Finchie got angry. Off he went into a huddle with Ted. Back they came. I was to do it in slow motion, with no harness, but with Finchie and Ted supporting me. Over I flipped. No problem.

'Now. Go it alone, Trade,' said Ted. 'And if you're in trouble, Finchie and I'll catch you. But for God's sake GO, man, or we'll be here all bloody night.'

The floor? Concrete! The crash mat? Thin rubber! They moved in.

'Shut your eyes, Trader,' from Ted. 'And when I say Ho…HuuuuP, reach for heaven.'

I heard 'Ho.' But before I heard 'HuuuuP' I felt an excruciating pain across the calves of my legs. Up and backwards I sprang. And my palms hardly seemed to touch the floor before I was back on my feet, light as a feather.

I didn't regret then, and haven't since, that Ted and Finchie used an old circus trick, whacking me on the calves with a thin cane, to make this Emu fly.

*The following dialogue takes place. It is in the form of an ad-lib with a gymnast planted in the audience.*

*Music: 'Dance of the Comedians' from Smetana's, 'The Bartered Bride.'*

PLANT: Come on, Trader, show us a back-flip.

TRADER: At my age? You're kidding.

PLANT: Come on. I'll spot you.

TRADER: Can you?

PLANT: Would I offer if I couldn't?

TRADER: (*Very dubious.*) Okay.

*PLANT comes up on stage.*

PLANT: Explode from your legs for lift off, keep your head tucked into your arms, extend your arms, rotate your hips, and GO FOR IT.

*TRADER goes for it, funks it on take off, is caught by the PLANT, goes again, does back-flip.*

*Music up, then fades out.*

# Caught Short

Peter Finch was the culprit responsible for my first appearance in theatre – an amateur production of *Hamlet* in a grotty hall in North Sydney.

'They're looking for someone to play a messenger,' said Finchie. 'Only four lines. Surely you can manage that?'

I was cast as the messenger who brings letters from Hamlet to Claudius. Dressing at the opening night, my tights concertina-ed in wrinkles all the way down my legs. So I got hold of a long length of tape to brace them up. After I'd put them on – an actor's trick this – I fixed large coins inside the tops as makeshift buttons. To these I secured the tape, winding it many times over my shoulders, round and round my waist, endlessly under my crotch…

By the time I'd finished I'd trussed myself up like Tutankhamun. All circulation had stopped and I could feel rigor mortis setting in. To make matters worse I was busting for a leak – my back teeth were under water.

The play by now was well on its way and coming up to my cue.

'I've got to get to the dunny,' I told Johnny Craig, who, like me, was waiting his entrance. 'Then you better put your skates on, mate,' said Johnny.

Seizing my letters from Hamlet, I just managed to get to the lavatory directly below the stage and cold and dank as Fingal's Cave.

I dropped Hamlet's letters on the floor, frantically unwound the tapes – the bloody tights had no fly so I had to lower them a bit – and, with enormous relief, let Nature take its course. Above me, the play droned on. How near was my cue? I listened. Laertes whinging on about Hamlet killing his old man. 'And so have I a noble father lost.' Shit!... I'm on!

Heaving up my tights I struggled to rewind the tapes, gave up half way, grabbed Hamlet's letters from the floor, stuffed them in my doublet and, forgetting it was strictly forbidden to pull the chain during performance because of the noise, flushed the ancient dunny – called Volcania.

*Deafening sound of a 1912 lavatory flushing.*

Loud guffaws came down to me from the audience.

Up the stairs I stumbled, my cue now passed, and saw that Johnny Craig wasn't in the wings waiting to go on as Osric. That wizard at improvising Shakespearean doggerel had seen his moment. *He* was on stage bowing to Claudius. He spoke:

'The messenger, my liege, was taken short
And thus delayed in making his report.'

I cut *him* short, hobbled on, my tights manacled to my ankles, penny coins rolling under the seats of the customers, and landed prostrate at the King's feet.

*Falls flat.*

'Letters, my Lord, from Hamlet,' I gasped. And withdrew from my doublet a large wadge of lavatory paper – in my panic I'd snatched it from the dunny floor instead of Hamlet's letters.

Wild ribald laughter from the audience
encouraged me to hand a sheet to the King.

*Tears off a sheet and hands it to CLAUDIUS.*

TRADER: This, to your Majesty…

CLAUDIUS: (*Horror struck.*) *This*…from Hamlet?

We were no longer in a play. This was vaudeville.
Johnny Craig, now well away, let his inspiration
flow:

'My Lord, these strange events take not amiss
For when your bladder's full you've got to piss
And if you, too, need urgently to go
Volcania's throne awaits you down below.'

That was it. Down came the curtain. Johnny and
I were sacked on the spot.

# My Night with Trixie

I wonder if any of you know that Cole Porter number from his old Broadway musical *Out of This World?*

*Sings three lines from it, ending with the line, 'I'm absolutely bursting with sex'.*

I was just twenty then – and *I* was bursting with sex, frustrated sex. I was still a virgin, believe it or not, and lusting after a feisty Sydney model called Trixie.

*Reveals photo of Trixie and kisses it.*

Oh Trix! You were to die for.

I was determined she would be my first consummated love. But buying my first condom threw me into a state of catatonic embarrassment.

'Steady on there, young Ron,' said Ernie Rundle the local chemist. 'Why don't you sit down for a minute.'

Sex was no stranger to Trix, so she was quick to say 'Yes' when I invited her to spend time that summer at our home, The Orchard. Mum, however, saw Trix as ninety miles of bad road.

A word about my mother. A ballerina in Diaghilev's first London season, she had danced as principal coryphée at the Met in New York and toured South America with Anna Pavlova. Pavlova, who always travelled first-class, sent Mum and the company steerage on an old tramp steamer. Some Peruvian prostitutes bound for Panama befriended Mum and she danced for them. In return they gave her a small dagger

similar to those the whores wore in their knickers.
Mum found this very handy for self-protection
when, a few weeks later, she arrived penniless in
New York. That was in 1919. In London in 1922
she married Dad who, despite his restless eye for
a pretty girl, was her mentor in life's game of love
and chance.

*Reveals photo of Mother.*

There's Mum in her brief and only appearance on
the silent screen in a film that starred Dad called
*The Breaking of the Drought.* Dad is among those
dubious lechers ogling Mum, but we could never
make out which one he was.

But back to Trixie. By the time she arrived at The
Orchard, looking like Mata Hari, Mum was well
prepared. She had invited two friends to stay,
Sybil, and Sybil's odious lover Ray Herkimer.
That pair, as Mum knew, believed that hard work
dulls a randy appetite. Egged on by her, they
cooked up fiendish schemes to keep Trixie and me
busy. They never left us alone for one second.

Mutual passion finally drove us to go for what
we desperately wanted in the great outdoors.
We planned the night. But dinner that evening
was endless. None of the prison warders seemed
tired. There was the washing up. Then a game of
cards. It was nearly one am before anyone made a
general move towards bed.

In my room I waited. Outside – bright moonlight
and silence except for the buzz of cicadas.
Inside – a symphony of nasal road-drilling from
the sleeping jailers told me I was clear for take-
off. Into the garden I sped and round to Trix's
window, a screwdriver in one hand, a ladder

under my arm. Up I shinned and scratched ever so lightly on the wire fly-screen fixed to the outside of the window.

Trixie, in a flimsy nightie, was raring to go.

'When I've got these bloody screws right out, give the fly-screen a shove,' I hissed. But the wooden frame holding it wouldn't shift. Trixie, frantic, tried to kiss me through the wire.

'Oh darling…my lovely beetle! For God's sake get it out,' she whispered.

'I can't get a grip on it,' I moaned back.

Suddenly the screen gave. Out shot Trixie, like an intoxicatingly perfumed human missile. I grabbed her. CRASH. Down went the ladder and us with it, arse over turkey, giggling and rolling over and over on top of each other in the soft grass.

'Who's that?' bawled Ray. Ray, by now at his window, had spied the ladder and fly-screen on the grass.

'Sybil, Sheila,' he yelled, 'it's those bloody kids.'

We shot out of that garden like a fart from a racehorse. I can still remember the feeling of reckless ecstasy at what lay ahead.

My special choice for our love-tryst was a gorgeous, low-lying jungle of clover about three-quarters of a mile away. But, Trix was never one for walking. And being barefoot didn't help.

'Ouuuuch! God! How much further?' she wailed as she trod on a bindie. 'C'mon, Trade, let's do it here.' Here being the stone gutter of an asphalt road.

When we at last reached the chosen spot, Trix streaked ahead, tore off her nightie, and flung herself naked into the clover. It was soaking wet.

'Shit,' she hissed.

'Don't worry, darl, I'll soon make your forget the dew,' I muttered, plunging my hand into my trouser pocket for the precious and most embarrassing purchase I'd ever made. But looking at it I was appalled…

'Trix, it's got a hole in it.'

'A hole?' she yelled. 'You're an arsehole!'

Slapping me an almighty wallop across the face, she snatched up her nightie, leapt to her feet, and vanished into the moonlight. A shimmering, white vision of unrequited lust.

# Smile Please

Soon after that embarrassing disaster I sailed for England.

I arrived in London to try my luck as an actor on a chilly May morning. Anxious for work, I phoned Britain's then most inventive play director, Tyrone Guthrie, who'd seen me act in Sydney. He generously wrote to the top West End management of those days, H M Tennent, and they invited me to audition for the Broadway production of Christopher Fry's play *The Lady's Not For Burning,* directed by John Gielgud.

This had been a huge success in London, with the leading parts played by Gielgud himself, Pamela Brown, and the young Richard Burton. The production was going to New York with the same cast, except for Burton who was off to play Henry V at Stratford. My audition – can you believe it? – was for Burton's role.

When I'd finished the audition, a tall bald man with a very large nose came forward to the front of the stalls.

*Reveals photo of John Gielgud.*

What a nose! Perfect casting for Cyrano de Bergerac. Yet he never played it.

'I'm John Gielgud. What's your name?'

'Ronald Faulkner, Sir.'

'Ronald? Oh God, what a dreary name.'

'In Australia I'm known by my nickname, Trader.'

'Trader? Wonderful! We'll bill you on Broadway as Trader. Welcome to the company.'

In New York, at an early rehearsal, Gielgud took me to one side.

'Oh dear. Richard had such a beautiful smile. You have those unfortunate crooked teeth. You really should do something about them.'

After the play had opened I did do something about them. Off I went to Dr Pfeiffer, a top New York orthodontist, who said he'd try his best to straighten them with a special appliance.

Over several weeks two small wire grids were made, like a miniature element in an electric kettle, one to go under my tongue, the other in the roof of my mouth. These grids were attached to hooks soldered on to metal bands. When Dr Pfeiffer finally fitted the bands, he hammered them down and cemented them on to my molars.

'Alrighty, Mr Faulkner. How does that feel?'

'I car spee properly. Mye outh's ired u ike a unky caye.'

'Say for me, "She sells sea shells on the sea shore."'

'Eshee eshells shee eshells o he hee hore.'

'Mr Faulkner, after an hour or so, to allow for subsidence, your articulation will sound just beautiful. Mr Gielgud will love it.'

I reeled into Fifth Avenue knowing I had to be speaking Christopher Fry's complicated verse to a packed house in two hours' time.

As the curtain rose, there I was, on stage as usual, writing at a medieval lectern. Gielgud appeared, framed in a large Gothic window. He paused on the ledge and called my name, 'Soul!...'

At this juncture I was supposed to say, with my back to him: 'And the plasterer...that's fifteen groats for stopping up the draught in the privy.'

What came out was, 'An er haster...ash heheen gwots hor oping hi hart i er hrivvy.'

From the Gothic window came an anguished 'Ohhhh!' The rest of the act was a nightmare. At the interval, as I bolted distraught from the stage, Gielgud called:

'Trader...Trader. Are you drunk?' He saw my eyes fill with tears. 'Dear boy, for God's sake. Just tell me. I won't be angry.'

'Ish a afiance to shatan my hore hee.'

'Oh my God. It's like something deformed. Quasimodo. We've got to get this frightful thing out quickly.'

Rushing me to his dressing room he called for Harry the stage carpenter and told him to bring his toolbag.

'I've only got these,' said Harry, and out of the bag came a hammer, pliers, and a chisel.

'Use them,' cried Gielgud, 'use any tool you've got. Use your screwdriver. But get that revolting contraption out before the audience ask for their money back.'

Harry tried desperately to prise down the top metal band. No luck. Then the bell went for the middle act. This, thank God, was almost entirely dialogue between Gielgud and Pamela Brown. I simply had to wash the floor. But, at the interval, it was back to Harry and cries of:

'Quickly, quickly!' from Gielgud.

Harry now wrestled with prising up the bottom band. It wouldn't budge. Then out of the blue, over the tannoy in my dressing room calling beginners for Act Three, came this:

'Miss Penny Munday has unfortunately become too ill with flu to continue. Her understudy will take over for the rest of the play.'

I staggered back for this last act, my mind in turmoil. Penny was playing the girl I was supposed to be in love with. We had an important love scene together – we were about to elope.

Up went the curtain with me on stage. And as Penny's replacement made her entrance – all of 6 feet to my 5 foot 10 – she seemed very unsteady on her feet. My first line, 'The crickets are singing well with their legs tonight,' sounded to me reasonably intelligible. But she fixed me with a stare of glazed amazement and started to giggle. To shut her up I planted a smacking kiss on her mouth. Whew! Brandy! Light a match and we'd both have gone up in flames.

On my next line, 'Oh Alison, I so love you. Are you afraid to come away?' she was supposed to bend down and lift up the back of her overskirt to make a hood, ready to elope. Up went her underskirt as well. Over her head went both skirts, blinding her, and revealing a shapely bottom clad in a pair of sexy red knickers.
A galvanised audience rippled with laughter.

From my bride-to-be (enveloped in her skirts, legs apart, and looking like a photographer with a tripod about to take a flash) burst an urgent whisper that carried well to the back of the dress circle:

'Where the hell am I? Why's everybody laughing? I'm as blind as a fucking bat.'

At that moment, one of Dr Pfeiffer's fittings sprang out and zapped itself on to my upper lip. And there it stayed.

For the rest of the play I was not only a man with a cleft palate. I was a man with a hare-lip.

# I Meet the Minotaur

Peter Hall once had the idea – never realised – of directing a play called *Bullfight*. He wanted me for the lead, a matador. So I went to Granada to learn about the role. There, I was befriended by Paco Velez, an habitué of Spanish café society, called a Tertulia. He introduced me to his tertulian amigos, all stalwarts of the Granadine establishment.

Paco told them I'd come to Spain to *be* a torero. I thought he was having them on, and they seemed to believe him. But as they offered to put me in touch with a famous ex-matador, Rafael Fandila, I didn't enlighten them. Rafael had been badly gored, and was now giving lessons to aspiring toreros. Each morning this pitifully crippled man would charge at me with a single bicycle wheel, its handlebars surmounted by a bull's head made of basketwork.

I became totally caught up in this. No longer interested in merely researching my role in *Bullfight*, I now made up my mind to try my hand as a matador. What the Tertulia thought I was there for, I now *was* there for.

Rafael showed me how to do some of the many different passes, including *the* most dangerous, the Veronica de Rodillas, where – to cape the bull as he charges – you swivel in a pirouette on both knees, and as he turns and charges back, your cape has to wipe his sweating snout, as Veronica wiped the face of Christ.

After six weeks of this, the Tertulia, led by Paco, came along to see my progress. Their response was friendly mockery.

*'Hombré! Que Torero! Que Maravilla! Será un gran torero de salon!'* –'A torero just about good enough to leap about in sequins in a nightclub.'

Confidential chat among the Tertulia now gave me time to nip off and get the box of Havana cigars I'd bought for Rafael. He'd refused any payment. But when I gave them to him, he looked at me as though I'd handed him a box of poop sticks.

Paco took me aside, 'Rafael ees very offended.'

'Why?' What have I done?'

'Th'only thanks he would rilly appreciáte ees for you to show heem that he hasn wasted hees time with you.'

'Look, I'll do anything he wants.'

'You min that?'

'Of course.'

'A man of hees word?' Paco solemnly put out his hand.

'Absolutely,' I shook it.

'What Rafael wants ees to see you in the ring confronting a live bull. He belivs you are riddi.' Christ! But to a Spaniard like Paco my word was sacrosanct.

For the next week I could think of nothing but fighting that live bull in some God-forsaken ring somewhere out of town...

The dreaded morning arrived. Dolores, the plum-ripe maid at the pension, brought me olives, sherry, and sausage called chorizo.

'*Macho hombre. Tienes que comer.*' – 'A macho lad like you must eat.' Down went the olives with a gollop of sherry…five minutes later up they came…rats deserting the sinking ship.

A knock at the door. The tailor with my made-to-measure bullfighter's suit. Behind him were three divine Granadine girls who quickly began the ritual of dressing me, the '*novillero*' – 'novice': grey striped trousers, white frilled shirt, short tight-fitting grey jacket, champagne-coloured suede boots and a wide dove-grey sombrero Cordobés. One of the girls, Rosario, spun me into an emerald-green cummerbund and fastened it tightly.

A 1930s Packard was waiting outside the pension, where a small crowd had gathered – the word had got around. From under the lid of the boot protruded the handles of several swords, with which I was clearly expected to despatch the bull. Someone handed me a bunch of red carnations – symbol of Spanish machismo. Amid shouts of '*Olé torero! Coraje! Vaya con Dios.*'– 'Go with God.' I was driven off.

Paco met me at the bullring and took me into the bullring patio. Along one of its white walls were three doors painted red. I peered through the first. A lavatory. Then through the next. Inside were an operating table and a tray laid out with surgical instruments. Against the back wall, discreetly covered by a black cloth, I could just see the outline of a coffin. In front of it, smiling pleasantly, was a white-coated surgeon.

'*Hola, hombre, tenga suerte.*' – 'Hello man, be lucky.'

I opened the third door and saw a little chapel.

Above the altar a painting of the Virgin, La Macarena, Our Lady of all Brave Toreros, gazed down at me compassionately. I mouthed a Hail Mary. Despite the heat of the day I was freezing.

'Are you riddi, Trahdare?' called Paco. My cuadrilla, my two assistants, lined up on either side of me.

A band struck up a paso doble, Gato Montes.

*Music on. TRADER speaks over, moving across stage like a torero entering the ring.*

We moved across the shadows of the patio, through an archway, and out into the blazing sunlight of the arena. The small ring was packed. Coloured shawls were draped along the barrera protecting the spectators. Behind them, I caught a glimpse of the three Granadinas who had dressed me.

*Music off.*

Rafael had said I was to go to the centre of the ring, look up to the President's box, raise my sombrero in salute and call '*Permiso*' – 'Permission to fight.' I went through that ritual in a trance.

From the President's box the keys of the toril, where the bull waited penned up, were thrown down to me. I managed to catch them and, as instructed by Rafael, threw them to one of my cuadrilla. He walked across the ring to the toril gate and slowly unlocked it.

The trumpet blasted for the bull to come out.

*Sound on, then off at end of trumpet call. Pause. Dead silence.*

Nothing happened. Only a rattling noise as the gate started to lift. Then stuck. Then dropped.

By now I could hear the Minotaur snorting. Ready for the kill, he was viciously kicking his pen.

The trumpet blasted a second time. This time up clanked the gate like a guillotine, right to the top. I felt giddy…nausea… I thought I was going to faint. I closed my eyes, just conscious of the soft thud of hooves coming across the sand. Closer and closer they came. Then suddenly stopped.

*Pause.*

I opened my eyes. There right in front of me was a tiny little bull-calf. Two large oranges were fixed on his nubby hornlets. He nuzzled my belly with his wet snout, blinked in the sun, and lay down at my feet. For the first time in the annals of bullfighting, Toro and Torero were evenly matched.

*TRADER turns away, then turns back.*

Spanish practical jokes can be very elaborate.

# Thwarted by Goliath

A very well known actress once cast a spell over me for seven years. The spell is long since broken but the bittersweet memory still lingers after a half a century.

Discretion prompts me to call her Marion Harkness. We met when she was twenty-one. We were acting in a play together. She was piquante and elusive. I was absolutely bewitched.

*Reveals photo too quickly for audience to see who it is, and places it with its back towards them.*

London audiences and critics praised her in superlatives. But Marion had a complaint that brought on bouts of nausea.

In the maze at Hampton Court I took her in my arms.

'I think I'm going to be sick,' she said.

She took me for a drive in her brand-new sports car. I went to kiss her.

'I think I'm going to be sick,' she said.

In Richmond Park, lying under a tree, I tickled her with a blade of grass.

'I think I'm going to be sick,' she said.

You can imagine what that did for my self-confidence, never strong at the best of times.

Well that was in the summer. By the autumn I was still getting nowhere. But I knew her dream was to live on a houseboat. I found her a beauty – the perfect love-nest – moored on Chelsea Reach.

I quickly rented a houseboat for myself moored practically next door.

Into this tragi-comedy a theatrical Goliath now makes his entrance.

*Reveals a photo of Laurence Olivier. Ad-libs briefly about him.*

He was to incite a feeling in me the French understand well – a compulsion to kill because of tormented love, to commit a *crime passionel.*

It all started soon after Marion and I became river-neighbours. I'd had to move to Stratford for the season to play Malcolm to *his* Macbeth. And on the afternoon of the opening night I was in the actors' pub, the Dirty Duck. A man asked if he might join me. We began to chat. He said he was on his way to the stage door to drop a note for Sir Laurence Olivier.

I told him I was an actor in the company and could save him the trouble. He gave me the note. It was on a plain card. The handwriting was Marion's. He'd met her at the Edinburgh Festival, and mentioned he was going to Stratford next day and she'd asked him to deliver the note.

Saying I'd see Sir Laurence got the card at once, I raced across the road to the comparative privacy of the Bancroft Gardens where I read it. It was a warm and loving message of good luck. No more. But, as Iago knew:

'Trifles light as air are to the jealous confirmations strong as proof of holy writ.'

Inflamed by no word from Marion myself, my imagination went berserk. Olivier, my hero – to whom I'd once confided my love for Marion –

was now my rival in love. You bastard, I thought, scavenging like a fruit-fly on the girl I worship. I tore back to the theatre and up the stairs to the star dressing-room.

Knock, knock. 'Larry?'

'Yes?'

'Could I disturb you for a moment?'

'Baby! A moment and no more. We're on in exactly forty minutes, and you've got to get made up, Cully.'

'I've got a message for you. A man in The Duck asked me to give you this.'

Olivier needed glasses to read. He reached for them, put them on, glanced quickly at the card, then watched me in the mirror.

There was a long pause.

'Ummmm!' he said. 'Little Harkness is a great actress.' I just waited. After an even longer pause he took off his glasses and rubbed his eyes.

'Can I give you a piece of advice? Malcolm. The way you're playing Malcolm.'

'Yes?'

'Having played it myself, twenty-eight years ago, it's one of Shakespeare's dreariest characters. Your only big scene is there to give Macbeth a rest before Dunsinane. But you do have a nice little speech at the end. And you're clowning it. Why, Baby?'

'Clowning it?'

'Go on say those last five lines.'

'This and what needful else
That calls upon us, by the grace of Grace,
We will perform in measure, time, and place:
So, thanks to all at once and to each one,
Whom we invite to see us crowned at Scooone!'

My operatic Scooone was like Olivier's: 'God for
Harry, England and St Geeooorge' in his film of
*Henry V.* Surely that would please him!

'Baby,' he said, 'you sound exactly like an air-raid
siren. If you do it that way tonight at the first night
the customers will piss themselves laughing. Is
that what you want?'

'How would you do it?'

'To see us *crowned* at Scone.'

He sat me down beside him and from his make-
up tray scooped out a blob of undertaker's wax,
a tiny ball of which he put on the tip of my nose,
and reshaped it.

'Now, Baby, you begin to look like Vivien's twin.'
He had switched to another of my roles that
season, Sebastian, twin-brother to Vivien Leigh's
Viola in *Twelfth Night.* He'd moulded my nose
with a little wooden spatula to make a perfect
retroussé identical to Vivien's.

*Reveals photo of Vivien Leigh, stands in profile against
it and tilts his nose to make it retroussé.*

'That's the spatula I used for the very first
performance of Richard III at the New Theatre
in London.' For a second he hesitated. 'Here,
Baby, keep it…and learn how to do a proper
nose.' Then, 'Christ! Out. Quick! We're on in five
minutes.'

I was halfway up the stairs to my dressing room clutching the historic spatula – treasured still, like a piece of the True Cross – before I realized how brilliantly he'd switched my mind away from Marion.

But the potentially explosive situation between Olivier, Marion and me was far from ending there. In my houseboat again, the Stratford season finished, I got to know the night watchman at the Chelsea boatyard – Ben Bowyang, a lizard-eyed mischief-maker, who spied on everyone who came and went. He knew on my passion for Marion. And confirmed my suspicions by telling me that she'd recently received a late night visit from Sir Laurence Olivier. I felt like a private in the French army discovering that his girl was being bedded by Napoleon. Crazed with jealousy, I was ready to flatten him the moment he set foot again on Marion's boat.

I'd made no bones about this to Ben.

'Trader,' he said one evening, 'Why don't ya give 'im a bunch of fives, or clock 'im wiv a bottle? Just the job.'

I was in such state I took him seriously. In the grip of an obsessive passion, I was capable of murder.

The moment to strike came at the end of a freezing January day when Ben told me Marion was expecting another visit from Sir Laurence. And that very night.

Now, at the top of the gangway leading to the houseboats in those days was a dirty great garbage bin. One of its handles had been torn off, leaving two holes. Long after dark I emptied the stinking contents into the river, climbed in, put the lid back on, and waited – using the holes to peep through.

Sure enough, after about half-an-hour, Goliath arrived and vanished down the hatch of Marion's boat.

I must have crouched in that bin for hours. A blinding icy wind whined in at me through my peep-holes. My teeth were chattering with nerves and cold. Eventually I had to get out to stretch my legs. Presently I saw a Bentley pull up on the opposite side of Cheyne Walk, and out stepped what looked like a very classy whore in a leopard-skin coat. Touting for customers, I thought. Or has she some pre-arranged assignation with *him* once he's finished with Marion? But after walking up and down for a bit, the leopard-skin beauty drove off.

I returned to my vigil in the garbage bin, and pulled down the lid. At last, through my peepholes, I saw two figures emerge on to the deck of Marion's boat, the arms of one encircling the dark outline of the other.

'Goodnight, my darling,' I heard Marion whisper.

Up I rose. Marion, glimpsing this bin-lidded apparition across Olivier's shoulder, shot back down her hatch and slammed it shut.

I lumbered forward, one hand behind me clutching an empty wine bottle. Olivier, not yet aware of me, made his way carefully up the gangplank. He saw me and stopped dead. In the grey dawn, there he stood, a very exhausted man in a bowler hat, a pin-striped suit and canary-yellow gloves, staring at me aghast, mouth open, speechless.

I moved in to savage him. His response threw me. He opened his arms wide. He was Jesus, forgiving and loving.

'Baby… Baby,' he crooned, unshaven, haggard, vulnerable.

I was lost. I tossed the bottle behind me into the Thames and flung out both *my* arms.

'Oh Larry, how lovely to see you!' I said. And there we swayed, clasped in a silent embrace on the rocking pontoon.

'Baby, what *are* you doing here?'

I floundered and lied desperately. 'I'm about to play a madman on TV. And I'm getting into character.'

He took my face between his hands. 'Well, let me tell you. You're a *very* convincing madman. You're going to be wonderful in the part. A definitive lunatic, Baby.' He kissed me on both cheeks and, looking beyond me, 'I've got to go. I see my car's waiting.'

Off he went, blowing me another kiss as he disappeared.

It had begun to snow. I just stood there.

Years later at a diner party given by Vivien Leigh shortly before she died, I told this story. Vivien knew about Larry and Marion anyway. Her face was a study.

'Oh Trader, jealousy was crucifying *both* of us. The leopard-skin 'whore' on the embankment was me.'

---

**Note:** Marion Harkness is, in fact, Dorothy Tutin, who died, sadly, on 6 August 2001.

# Wartime Morning

Now let me take you back to re-live a morning in 1940 that I've never been able to forget.

When I was twelve or thirteen I used to visit my Uncle Jim, Aunt Lily and cousin Rosemary in the Sydney suburb of Balmoral. The house was on a hill, with a majestic view of the entrance to Sydney Harbour.

On his veranda Uncle Jim had a telescope on a tripod. Hours of my youth were spent gazing through this at the daily traffic of the great ships, so I soon knew the details of nearly every vessel that came and went.

One wartime Saturday morning I was at Uncle Jim's swotting maths. I wanted to be out there in the surf with my mates, riding the big white breakers on my old wooden surfboard.

Drifting into a daydream I heard, or thought I heard, away in the distance, a band playing what I now know was Verdi's *Grand March* from *Aida*.

*Hums it.*

An urgent voice outside my door brought me back to reality: 'Ronnie, Ronnie, come quickly! You'll never see anything like this ever again.'

I rushed out. Everyone else was heading for the veranda. From there we saw a tremendous spectacle. Steaming in single line ahead out of Sydney Harbour, all painted battleship grey, were the *Queen Mary*, the P&O liners *Mooltan*, *Narkunda*, *Chitral*, *Comorin*, *Strathmore* and *Strathnaver*, and the Orient liners *Orion*, *Orcades*, *Otranto*, *Oronsay*.

With them as escorts, led by the flagship Australia, were the cruisers *Canberra* and *Adelaide*, the sloops *Swan* and *Yarra* and four V and W destroyers, *Waterhen, Voyager, Vampire* and *Vendetta,* with their flotilla leader *Stuart.*

The crews of these ten warships, in dazzling white, stood motionless on deck in the blazing sunshine. On the quarter deck of the *Australia* a band was playing the music that had entered my daydream.

On the troopships were thousands of Australian and New Zealand diggers. They were packed not only on the decks, but on the funnel ladders, the davits, the ratlines, the taffrails, up in the crows-nests – countless cheering men, dressed in khaki, waving their familiar slouch hats.

On Uncle Jim's veranda we watched transfixed. This vast armada, we learned later, was taking two Divisions to help hold Tobruk and the North African desert against Rommel, and had been assembling over some time in the upper reaches of Sydney Harbour, out of sight.

These ships suddenly coming into view round Middle Head seemed to us to have appeared from nowhere. But this monumental exodus was obviously no secret to everyone. On that wide blue expanse of Sydney Harbour, looking like toys in comparison, floated every kind of smaller craft from ferry steamers to canoes. Wives, mothers, daughters, sisters, sweethearts, children, the elderly, had taken to the water to wave goodbye.

And on that clear, cold, sunny morning, a brisk North Easterly carried across to us on our veranda, along with the cheers and the music of the band, the sound of ships' horns blowing their farewells. All this was awesome and glorious. I was just a kid, but I knew that many of those boys would never come back.

It was my first awareness of what the war – until then so very far away – was really about.

# Will You Join the Dance?

I first saw him when I was twenty-three. He was holding London audiences spellbound at the Cambridge Theatre, presented by Peter Daubeny. Among his many lovers, they tell me, were Ava Gardner, Gina Lollabrigida – and the Duke of Windsor.

Who was he? The flamenco icon, Antonio – the greatest dancer Spain produced in the twentieth century.

*Reveals photograph.*

Waist like a wasp and a tongue like its sting.

The moment I saw him dance I resolved to learn flamenco myself – not to be a dancer, but to develop physical expressiveness and freedom as an actor.

'Good God, Trader, why learn flamenco?' said Olivier. 'British actors look ridiculous dancing.'

Undaunted, I went to Madrid to learn flamenco at its roots. There I sought out a maestro, Diego Marin. Years earlier he'd danced with a nail sticking up in his shoe, the wound had turned gangrenous and they'd cut off his leg. From a wheelchair he taught me style. How to dance flamenco *above* the waist, and how to make a lyrical gesture macho, never camp.

*Demonstrates briefly.*

From Diego Marin I moved on to the Sacromonte caves of Granada to learn from the gypsies. There a beautiful gypsy girl, Almudena, taught me another aspect of style.

'*Hombre! Que haces? Porque me mires asi? No me mires tan fija. Si quieres ligar lanza mirar.*' –

'Man! Why do you stare at me when you dance with me? If you want to turn a woman on when you dance with her, *gaze* at her. By staring you lose sensuality. Now dance with me and gaze at me.'

*Demonstrates.*

What an insight that lesson was.

Then, back in Madrid for a spell, came the event which vindicated all I'd been taught. At a lunch party thrown for Anthony Steel, who was filming there, he came over to me.

'I hear the Aussie flamenco dancer is making great progress,' he said. 'Look, I want you to meet a friend. Come with me. Now. It's your chance of a lifetime.' He said no more but drove me across Madrid to a palatial building. Inside he left me burning with curiosity. Spanish music was playing in the distance.

*Music on, very softly: Falla's 'Three-Cornered Hat'.*

Presently, back Anthony came and led me to a large room of baroque splendour. On a sofa, dressed from head to foot in scarlet, lounged a young man, delicately fingering a long black cigarette holder.

I stared.

'You're Antonio! It was you I saw dancing in London like a god.'

*Music off.*

'Yeth, Darlinc. When I danth badly I danth better than anywan in the world...and when I danth well,

I danth like Jesuth Christ. And I hear you too
danth the flamehnco. Well, the actor who danth
the flamehnco is now going to danth for me!'

I protested I was wearing a double-breasted suit,
braces and flat shoes. He merely shrugged.
I pleaded that without a guitarist I hadn't
Buckley's chance of putting on any kind of a show.

Moraito Chico, a famous gypsy guitarist, suddenly
materialised as if by magic.

I struggled through my dance, Farruca. Finished
it. Silence. Spain's dancing idol covered his face
with his hands and peeped at me through his
fingers. All I could see was one gleaming eye.

'Darlinc! You danth like a horth!'

Humiliated, I made for the door. He did nothing
until I opened it. Then:

'Darlinc, not a *cart* horth. Come back. All is
forgiven.'

Six months went by. Antonio was in London for
another dazzling season, this time at the Coliseum.
I was asked to a party after the first night. There
was dinner. Then party games.

'I *love* games,' said Antonio, 'if *I* choose the game.'

Everybody was told to sit around wherever they
could find a space. Someone asked Antonio what
the game was going to be.

'Trader is going to danth Farruca for os.'

As before, I was wearing a double breasted suit,
braces and flat shoes. But since my return to
London I had really sweated on that dance to give
it some semblance of style.

Moraito Chico started to play. By the end of my dance I knew I hadn't done too badly.

'Do you have a traje de Baile?' asked Antonio. A 'traje de Baile' is the tight, narrow-waisted, chest-high trousers, frilled shirt, short jacket and boots worn at that time by the 'Bailaor', the male dancer.

'Yes?'

'Good. I invite you as an actor to dance your solo with my company on our last night at the Coliseum.'

Was he throwing me to the lions for his own amusement? Did it matter?

'I'll have a go,' I said.

Before curtain-up on that last night I went to Antonio's dressing-room and told him I was anxious not to finish the Vuelta, the fast double spin that ends my particular Farruca, with my bum to the audience.

'Darlinc, your bum is your bes feature.'

*Reveals cartoon of Torero in the bullring, who just avoids being gored by the bull.*

'But if you want to give the audience secon best, have a word with the Veergin Mary, and she'll turn you roun the rih way.'

I was to come on at the very end, so I had the whole evening to get the shakes. I'd be on cold with no rehearsal, frighteningly inexperienced, in front of nearly three thousand people.

*Picks up flamenco boots. Speaks while putting them on.*

These are the old boots I wore for that performance – handmade by a famous flamenco bootmaker.

*Looks at the soles and reads.*

Gallardo, Madrid, 1959 – still visible.

I thought of making a bolt for it. But, mesmerised, I watched the finale from the wings. The entire company were gathering flamboyance in a steady crescendo. Suddenly, Antonio stopped the show and held up his hand. The audience waited, pin-still.

'Ladies and Gentlemen, tonigh I harve weting in thee weengs a green man, green he is with terror, green like you would be if I ask any one of you to come up here an danth with os. Thees poor man is so frighten that two peoples is holding him op. Because, he eesn't reeli a danther of flamenco. He ees an English actorr. But he loves thee danth, and he feels thee danth like I do. And so he weel danth Farruca.'

I walked on to the stage. Sixty of Spain's top guitarists, dancers and singers were lined up behind me, all hoping to God I wouldn't let them down, whispering:

'*Que te coge El Duende! Hombre suerte!*' – 'Good luck!'

Moraito Chico came up close:

'Trahdare, don' worri...we'll follow you with the music whatever you do.' The company began to clap out the rhythm...the Palmas. The guitars started to play.

Away I went.

*Music in loud. He dances, ending with fast spin. Music off.*

Within seconds we were all – the entire company – bowing to the audience. The house was on its feet. On to the stage flew red carnations, shoes, combs, even a suspender belt – which Antonio caught, kissed, clutched to his heart, rolled up and threw back.

Finally the company exploded into a gypsy Bulerias with me joining in. As it finished Antonio – a featherweight – leapt on my shoulders and we all swept off into the wings.

As we went he whispered in my ear, 'Well, darlinc, like I said before, you danth like a horth. But tonigh you were a *rathe* horth.'

# Lines in the Sand

I'll finish, briefly, with a meeting I once had in France.

One day on a beach at Golfe Juan in the South of France, I met Pablo, Diego, Jose, Francisco de Paula, Juan Nepomuceno, Maria de los Remedios, Crispin Crispiniano de la Santisma, Trinidad, Ruiz – Picasso.

*Reveals photo of Picasso. Ad-libs briefly about him.*

He was squatting on his haunches, doodling in the damp sand. He looked exactly like a burnished brown satyr.

'Well worn but worn well,' as the old Kiwi boot polish advert used to say.

The most striking thing about him was his eyes. They shone like black opals. And as he doodled, those black opals kept staring at a long row of German oldies sunbathing on the shore. They were lying in a straight line, breathing in unison, stripped, oiled, fat bellies sunny-side up, like grounded white balloons.

I started to laugh. Picasso turned to me. He spoke in French:

'You wouldn't find them funny if you'd lived in Paris through the Nazi occupation.'

His French had strong traces of his Andaluz origin.

'I'm better at Spanish than French,' I said, 'and I can just understand Andaluz.'

'*Y como?*' – 'How come?'

'I learned to dance flamenco from the Sacromonte gypsies.'

'*Porque*?' – 'Why?'

I told him of my flamenco odyssey, and of my lessons with the great Diego Marin who'd lost one of his legs.

Picasso roared with laughter:

'*Hombre! Tu eres un payaso.*' – 'You're a clown. Only in Spain could a British actor learn to dance flamenco from a man with one leg.'

He knelt and drew in the sand a one-legged man and me dancing wildly together. He worked like lightning, with a strong, stubby finger...just a few strokes...and there it was...conjured up in the sand...my likeness, unmistakable.

With a flourish he signed, '*Payaso y Bailaor con una pierna*' – 'Clown and one-legged bailaor' – Picasso.

Then he winked. And at that moment a small wave broke across the sand – and washed the image away.

*The End.*

Printed in the USA
CPSIA information can be obtained
at www.ICGtesting.com
LVHW020945171024
794056LV00003B/977